Kelp Forests

Contents

- About Kelp — 2
- Kelp Fronds — 10
- The Underwater Forest — 14
- Home and Hiding Place — 16
- A Source of Food — 18
- A Commercial Industry — 20
- The Price of Pollution — 22
- Glossary — 24
- Index — 24

Text by Stanley L. Swartz
Photography by Robert Yin

DOMINIE PRESS
Pearson Learning Group

About Kelp

Giant kelp forests are beautiful underwater **marine environments**. Kelp is one of the fastest growing plants on Earth. Some types of kelp can grow almost twelve inches in one day.

◀ Scuba Diver in a Kelp Forest

Giant kelp is the largest marine plant. Kelp plants are found mostly in shallow water of twenty to eighty feet. They live in water throughout the world.

◄ Giant Kelp

Kelp plants do not have a root system. They have what is called a holdfast. This is a mass of branches that **anchors** each plant.

◄ A Kelp Plant Holdfast

All parts of the kelp plant use photosynthesis. This is how plants change **carbon dioxide** and water into sugar and oxygen. The plant does this using sunlight.

◀ Kelp Forest Reaching for Sunlight

Kelp Fronds

The kelp **fronds**, or leaves, are closest to the surface. They get the most amount of sunlight. The fronds also take **nutrients** from the water.

◀ Kelp Fronds

Gas-filled **bladders** keep the fronds afloat. Kelp is very **flexible**. It gently sways with the **currents** of the water.

◀ Scuba Diver Deep in a Kelp Forest

The Underwater Forest

There are several layers in a kelp forest. The canopy layer is closest to the water's surface and receives the most sunlight. The middle layer receives less light. The floor level gets the least amount of sunlight.

◀ Kelp Forest Floor

Home and Hiding Place

Giant kelp forests are home to many animals. Kelp is protection for some animals. It is also a hiding place for **predators**.

◄ A Protective Cover of Kelp

A Source of Food

After a storm, kelp is often washed onto the shore. This provides food and shelter for birds and other animals. Kelp is an important source of food, both in and out of the water.

◀ Marine Life in a Kelp Forest

A Commercial Industry

Kelp is also an important commercial industry. Kelp is used in many kinds of food. Drug companies also use it.

◀ Diver in Sunlit Kelp Forest

The Price of Pollution

Over the years, kelp forests all over the world have become smaller. **Pollution** has damaged many of them. Scientists are working to find ways to **preserve** these beautiful underwater wonders.

◄ Fragile Underwater Forest

Glossary

anchor:	To hold in place
bladders:	Bodily sacs that store liquid or gas
carbon dioxide:	A colorless, odorless gas
currents:	The steady flow of water
environments:	Surroundings; the settings where animals or people live
flexible:	Able to bend without breaking
fronds:	Large leaves divided into many thin sections
marine:	Relating to the sea
nutrients:	Natural food that helps plants and animals grow
pollution:	Something that hurts the natural environment
predators:	Animals that hunt, catch, and eat other animals
preserve:	To save; to protect from harm

Index

bladders, 13

canopy layer, 15
carbon dioxide, 9
currents, 13

fronds, 11, 13

holdfast, 7

nutrients, 11

oxygen, 9

photosynthesis, 9

pollution, 23
predators, 17

root system, 7

scientists, 23
sugar, 9